Google Cloud Platform from the very beginning

Jerry N. P.

Subjects include: google cloud platform, compute server, networking server, storage server, database services, big data server, machine learning, identity services, security services, gcp, google cloud, creating account, cloud sql, google bigquery, SSDs, cloud DNS, google platform, google cloud, database server hardware, platform strategy.

Contents

Introduction

Companies are generating data in huge volumes every day. Some of this data is sensitive and if exposed to unauthorized individuals, the company can go through a hard time, which can even lead to closure of the company. Companies also need to extract intelligence from their data. This is good for evidence-based decision making. The Google Cloud Platform is a good cloud computing platform providing its users with features that can be used for such tasks. This book guides you on how to accomplish various tasks on the Google Cloud Platform. Enjoy reading!

Chapter 1- What is Google Cloud Platform (GCP)?

Google Cloud Platform (GCP) is a set of cloud computing services provided by Google. These services run on the same infrastructure that Google uses for the internal end products. Other than the management tools, GCP also provides a set of modular cloud services which include machine learning, data storage, computing and data analytics. The cloud is a good way of keeping data secure. It also provides us with servers that are dynamically scalable. The cloud also provides us with a faster computation as well as remote access to data and services. You will find so many cloud providers in the market. However, the GCP stands out for a number of reasons. It is the leading cloud platform in terms of providing its users with flexible pricing terms. Most cloud platforms do not provide their users with the flexibility that they need. GCP makes it easy for users to scale up and down at their convenience. It also provides Custom Machine Types which you can use to create custom machine types that are customized according to your needs at a great discount, even up to 50%. The GCP also supports Big Data Analytics, making it easy for you to perform analysis on your data. The GCP platform is server less, which is a new feature that helps us avoid the complexity of managing servers and back-end APIs, data processing jobs, ETL, databases etc. GCP simply provides a collection of cloud services. It hosts a number of services including:

- Compute
- Application development
- Storage

These Google cloud services can be accessed by cloud administrators, developers as well as other IT professionals. The access can be done via dedicated network connection or via the public internet.

Creating an Account

For you to be able to use the GCP services, you must first create an account. You are provided with an option of creating a free account on GCP. You will be given a credit worth $300 which you can spend for 12 months.

You are required to give details of your credit card, but you will not be charged extra once the trial period expires or once you exhaust the $300 credit.

To sign up for this free account, open the following URL: https://console.cloud.google.com/getting-started

You will be taken to the following page:

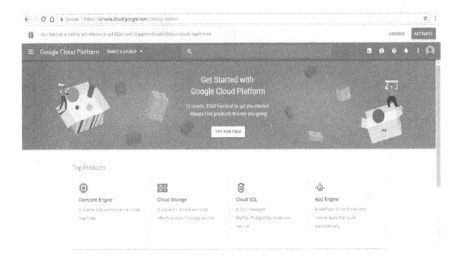

Click the "TRY FOR FREE" button.

You will be taken to a new page where you will have to provide a number of details.

Try Cloud Platform for free

Country

American Samoa ▼

Acceptances

Please email me updates regarding feature announcements, performance suggestions, feedback surveys and special offers.

○ Yes
○ No

I agree that my use of any services and related APIs is subject to my compliance with the applicable Terms of Service. I have also read and agree to the Google Cloud Platform Free Trial Terms of Service.

Required to continue

○ Yes
◉ No

AGREE AND CONTINUE

Privacy policy | FAQs

Fill in all your details then click the blue button written "AGREE AND CONTINUE".

In the next page, you will have to choose whether you are creating a business or individual account. Choose the right one based on your requirements. Of course, the business account will have more features compared to the individual account.

Enter your credit card details then precede. Your billing details will be setup.

Next, you will get a welcome message, showing that you have signed up successfully:

○ **Google** Cloud Platform

Welcome Nicholas!

Thanks for signing up for the 12-month free trial.

We've given you $300 in free trial credit to spend. If you run out of credit, don't worry, you won't be billed until you give your permission.

GOT IT

Click the "GOT IT" message to leave the dialog. You will have successfully signed up for a free GCP account. Congratulations!

The dashboard shows the various services that are provided by the GCP. You can start any of the services that you need and begin to use them.

Chapter 2- Google Cloud Services

The GCP provides its users with a number of services. These services run on the same platform as the Google's end-user products like Gmail, Google Search, YouTube and Google Photos. Let us discuss the services offered by GCP:

Compute Services

The GCP provides a number of scalable computing options. It comes with highly customizable virtual machines that you can edit to meet your needs and options. You may choose to deploy your code either directly or via containers. The following are the components of Google Compute service:

Google Compute Engine

The work of this is to deliver the virtual machines that are running in the innovative data centers of Google and worldwide fiber network. The Compute Engine virtual machines are well known for their ability to boot up quickly. They have local disk options and high-performance persistence that helps them offer a consistent performance.

Google App Engine

This is a platform used for building web applications with high scalability and IoT backends. The App Engine is capable of scaling the application automatically depending on the traffic that is received. It comes with built-in services and APIs like NoSQL, Datastores, Memcache and API for authentication, which is all common to most of the applications.

Google Kubernetes Engine

This is a cluster manager and a balanced system that helps you to run your Docker containers. The kubernetes engine is responsible for scheduling your containers into the cluster, keeping them healthy and automatically managing them depending on your requirements.

Google Cloud Container Registry

This is a Docker repository that is compatible with the common continuous delivery systems. It is a private repository.

Networking Services

Networking is one of the services that are provided by the Google Cloud Platform, and the most modern networking services are used for this purpose. It is made up of the following components:

Cloud Virtual Network

The various GCP resources can be connected to one another via a Google-owned global network, and they can also be isolated from one another via their Virtual Private Cloud (VPC) Network. The following are the steps necessary for the creation of a VPC network:

On the dashboard of your GCP account, click the "Navigation Menu" button located on the top left corner of the window:

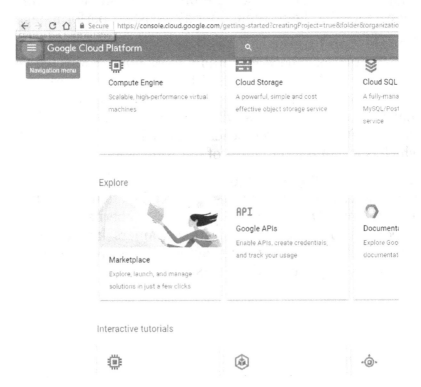

Navigation will appear. Scroll downwards and choose the option for "VPC network".

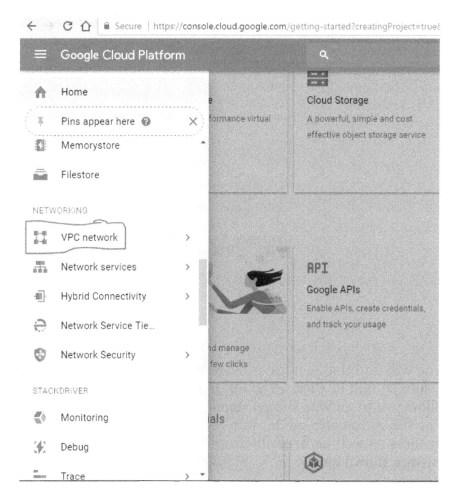

In the next page, click the button written "CREATE VPC NETWORK". A new page will be opened where you should provide details of the network, include the name and its description.

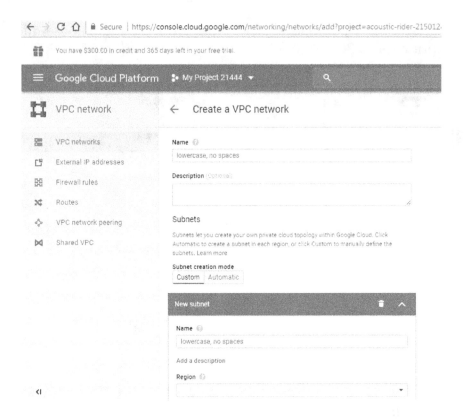

You will find that you are provided with the option of creating a subnet, that is, Custom or Automatic. The Custom mode will allow you to enter a subnet name, region and the IP address. For the Automatic mode, you will be provided with a list of subnets as well as firewalls from which you can choose. The two are shown below:

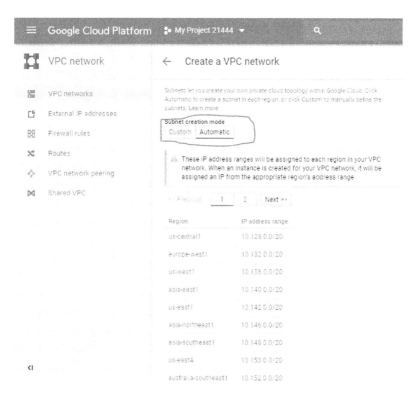

In the next step, you will be required to choose the routing mode, which can be Regional or Global, which will be determined by what you need. Once you are done with feeding the details, click the "Create" button located at the bottom and the VPC will be created.

Cloud Load Balancing

This is the tool responsible for allowing us to scale our apps based on our requirements. Your Compute machine resources should be balanced in either single or multiple regions and closer to the users so that their high availability requirements may be met.

Cloud Content Delivery Network (CDN)

It uses the globally distributed edge caches of Google to accelerate the process of content delivery of applications and websites that are served out of the Google Compute Engine. The Cloud CDN also reduces the network latency, reduces serving costs and offloads the origins.

Google Cloud Interconnect

The purpose of the Google Cloud Interconnect is to allow the cloud platform customers to establish a connection to Google via the enterprise-grade connections with a higher availability and low network latency compared to the current internet connections.

Google Cloud DNS

This is a reliable, managed authoritative and scalable DNS (Domain Naming System) service that runs on the same infrastructure as Google. It has a high availability; low latency and it provides you with a cost-effective way of making your services and application available to users.

Storage and Database Services

This provides the GCP users with a storage facility. It is made up of the following components:

Google Cloud Storage

This provides a unified offering throughout the Google spectrum. It has the capability of handling both live data and cloud archival solutions.

Cloud SQL

This is a fully managed database service that fastens the process of setting up, maintaining, managing and administering relational MySQL as well as PostgreSQL databases in the Google cloud.

Cloud Bigtable

This tool provides a NoSQL database that is massively scalable. It is well suitable for high throughput and low latency workloads. It can be integrated so well with other common big data tools like Spark and Hadoop. It also comes with support for the industry standard, open source, HBase API.

Google Cloud Datastore

This tool provides us with a high scalable, elastic document-oriented database as a service. This means that the goal of the Cloud Datastore is to store your data in the form of documents.

Persistent Disk

This is a block storage service with a high scalability that is good for container storage and virtual machines. The price for this service is not proportional to the high quality performance it offers.

Big Data Services

These are services that can be used for data analysis. They include the following:

Google BigQuery

This is a low cost, fully managed analytics data warehouse provided in the Google Cloud Platform.

Google Cloud Dataproc

This is a managed Hadoop and Spark service that is highly used for processing big datasets using the open and powerful tools available in Apache big data ecosystem.

Google Cloud Datalab

This is an interactive notebook good for exploration, collaboration, analysis and visualization of data. It is integrated with Google Cloud Machine Learning and BigQuery to provide an easy and quicker access to the key data processing services.

Google Cloud Sub/Pub

This is a large scale, server less, real time, reliable messaging service that can allow you to send and receive messages between any independent applications.

Machine Learning Services

These are services that provide machine learning capabilities. They include the following:

Cloud AutoML

This is a set of machine learning products that provide developers with only a limited machine learning knowledge with a platform where they can train high quality machine learning models by leveraging the Neural Architecture Search technology provided by Google.

Google Cloud TPU

This is a family of a number of hardware accelerators designed and optimized by Google to scale up and speed up machine learning workloads for inference and training that have been programmed with TensorFlow.

Google Cloud Machine Learning Engine

This engine provides you with a way of building large scale, sophisticated machine learning models covering a wide set of scenarios including building sophisticated image classification and regression models.

Identity and Security Services

This is an important service in the Google Cloud Platform as it is responsible for ensuring that your data is secured through encryption. It is made up of the following components:

Google Cloud Identity and Access Management

The IAM is responsible for allowing the administrators to control who is allowed to access and use which resources, providing an efficient and centralized way of managing the Google Cloud resources.

Cloud Security Scanner

This is a scanner that scans for web security by checking for the common vulnerabilities in the App Engine applications. Examples of such vulnerabilities include Flash injection, cross-site-scripting, insecure libraries and mixed content (HTTP in HTTPS).

Management and Developer Tools

The GCP comes with a number of management tools. These tools are used for monitoring the services debugging, finding errors and tracing the services.

An example of a management tool is the stack driver which provides a real-time monitoring and logging in the GCP. There are other useful management tools provided in the platform. The tools can be used for diagnostic purposes.

The GCP also provides you with a set of developer tools that makes it easy and quicker for you to develop brand new applications.

The Google Cloud SDK is an example of a developer tool. It is simply a set of tools and libraries that one can use for management of computing resources and applications that are hosted on the Google Cloud Platform. With cloud SDK, you are provided with interactive command line tools for management of your virtual machines your deployments and your cloud SQL instances.

Those are the various services that are provided by the Google Cloud Platform.

Chapter 3- Google App Engine

This is a platform that allows you to develop applications and run them on the Google Cloud Platform infrastructure. You can use it to create a multi-tiered web application from scratch or for hosting a static website. You can also use it to build mobile backends.

The good thing with the App Engine is that it scales automatically based on the traffic it receives, meaning that you will only pay for those resources you have used. Some of its features include health checks, load balancing and application logging, which provide you with a faster way of deploying your mobile and web applications.

The App Engine works together with other popular tools including Git, IntelliJ, Eclipse, Pycharm and Jenkins. This means that you are provided with the ability to use the tools that you like without having to change your workflow.

Creating a New Project

For you to be able to use the Google tools for your app or website, you should first create a new project on the Google Cloud platform. You must have a Google account to be able to do this. Follow the steps given below:

On the main dashboard of your GPC account, click the Navigation Menu button then scroll downwards to the section for "COMPUTE". From that section, click "App Engine" then choose "Dashboard".

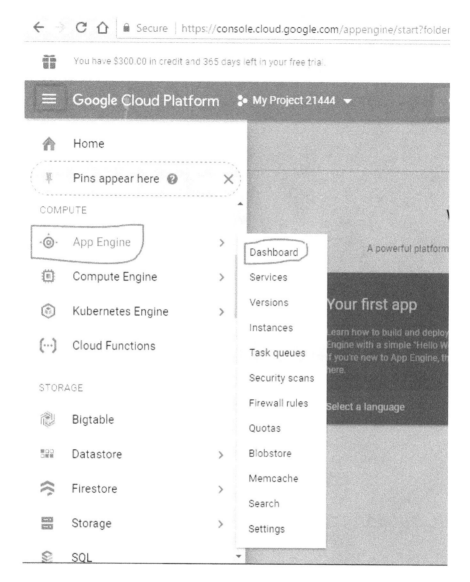

You will be taken to a new page from where we can proceed towards creating a new project.

We need to create a new project. In my case, I had created a project earlier, but I don't want to use it for this task, so I have to create a new one. If this is the case with you, click the drop down to the right of the project name at the top.

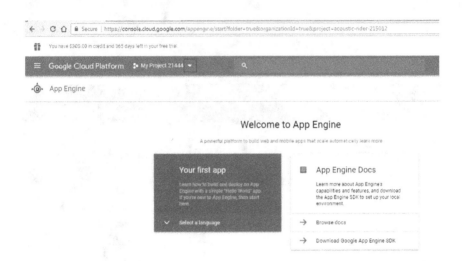

New window will popup. On the popup, click the "NEW PROJECT" button located at the top right corner.

Give the project a name then click the "Create" button. Congratulations, you will have created a new project successfully.

Creating an application

Every Cloud Platform project should only have one App Engine application. We can now prepare the app for the project.

You should have a sample application that you can publish. If you don't have it, you can find one online. Download it onto your computer. In my application folder, I have the "website" folder and the "app.yaml" file. The "app.yaml" file has the configuration details for the application. The content for the website is inside the "website" folder". The landing page for this should be named "index.html", but it can take any form that you want.

The configuration file, that is, "app.yaml" tells the App Engine how to map the URLs to the static files.

Publishing an application

We have already created our project and our project files have been assembled. It is now time for us to publish them. Follow the steps given below:

Begin by opening the Google Cloud Shell. You can access it on the following URL:

https://console.cloud.google.com/cloudshell/editor

Drag your project folder from your computer into the left pane of the page:

At the bottom of this window, there is a command line. This is where you should run the commands necessary for deployment of the application. Begin by running the following command:

gcloud config set project samplesite

```
nicholassamuel1107@cloudshell:~$ gcloud config set project samplesite
Updated property [core/project].
nicholassamuel1107@cloudshell:~ (samplesite)$ █
```

Run the cd (change directory) command to navigate to the project folder. In my case, the project folder has the name "sample-app", so I run the following command:

cd sample-app

```
nicholassamuel1107@cloudshell:~ (samplesite)$ cd sample-app
nicholassamuel1107@cloudshell:~/sample-app (samplesite)$ █
```

At this point, you are ready to deploy your application. Deploy means uploading the app to the App Engine. Just run the following command:

gcloud app deploy

Type in a number to choose a region in which you want the application located.

Confirm by typing "Y" for "Yes".

To see the website online, just open your-project-id.appspot.com on your browser. For example, our project is sample site, so we should open:

samplesite.appspot.com.

Chapter 4- Identity Access Management in Google Cloud

You may have many projects in your Google cloud that are accessed by many users. You need to be able to specify who can do what and on which resource. This can be done via the IAM (Identity Access and Management) system provided by the Google Cloud Platform. This system gives you a centralized control and visibility that you need to control your Google cloud resources. The implementation of the cloud IAM is a continuous, multi-step process. You first need to configure both the users and groups. You can then decide on whether to create functional roles, and then assign them to users. You must also determine whether the pre-defined roles that are offered by the GCP meet your requirements. If they don't, you have to create custom ones. You should test your IAM policies and revisit them on a frequent basis to ensure that they meet your needs. You can use the fine-grained Cloud IAM roles to grant different levels of access to the resources to the different users. There are various ways through which you can manage the user roles on the Google Cloud Platform. You can do this via the GCP Console, REST API, gcloud command-line tool, or via client libraries. The easiest method to do this is via the GCP console. I am assuming that you have created a project. If not, please do so following the steps we had discussed previously.

Adding a Member to a Project

We need to demonstrate how you can add a new member to a project then grant them an IAM role. Follow the steps given below:

On the dashboard of your GCP account, click the button for Navigation Menu.

Click "IAM &admin: then choose "IAM".

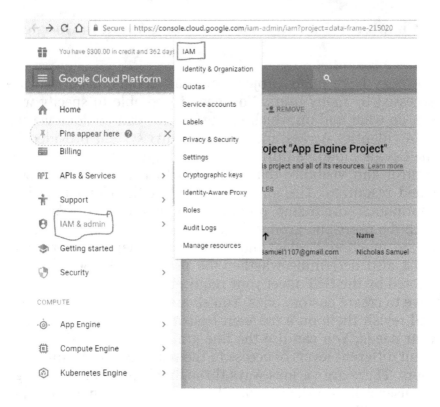

This will take you the page for the project that you have created. It is from here that you can add a member to the project.

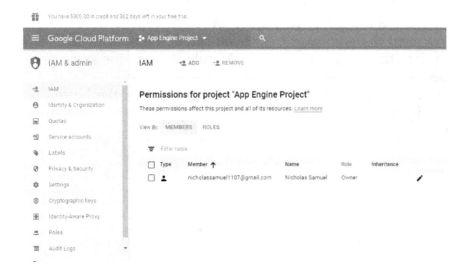

The page shows the current members for the project, plus their roles.
To add a new member to the project, click the "ADD" button located at the top:

You will be taken to a new page where you are allowed to add in new members to the project. Note that you are only allowed to choose an active email account for the user. The page also allows you to choose the role of the user. Some of the available roles include the owner, editor, browser and viewer. If you point at any of these, you will be notified of the privileges they will have on the project.

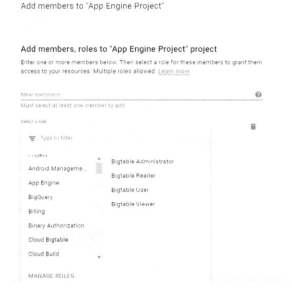

Here, you should choose the roles based on the GCP service that you use.

If you are using the Stackdriver Logging, choose "Logging" then "Logs Viewer".

If you are using the Compute Engine service, choose "Compute Engine" then "Compute Instance Admin".

If you are using the App Engine, choose "App Engine" then "Add Engine Admin".

If you are using the Cloud Storage, choose "Storage" then "Storage Admin".

Enter the email address of the new member, choose their role then click the "SAVE" button located at the bottom of that page. The good thing is that you are allowed to add more than one member to the project at once.

After clicking the SAVE button, you will be taken back to the project page, and you will find that the new members appear on the list. Their role will also be visible.

That is it; you have known how to add a new member to your project and granted them an IAM role.

Granting Other Roles

A user must not have one role in a project. It is possible for the user to have more than one role on the same project. Let us demonstrate how you can grant such additional roles to the user we have just created above:

Begin by clicking the Navigation Menu button from the main dashboard, choose "IAM & admin" then choose "IAM".

Ensure that you are in the project for which you need to add additional roles to the user.

Choose the member to whom you want to grant additional roles.

To the left of that users email address, click their checkbox to activate it. Move to the right and click the Edit icon which looks like a pen/pencil.

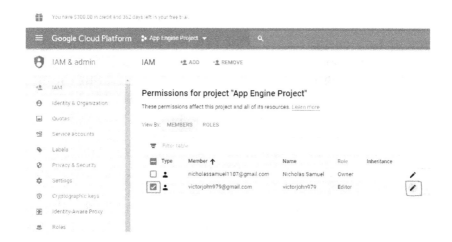

Click the icon will open a page from where you can add an additional role. Their current role will also be shown.

Click the button written "ADD ANOTHER ROLE".

This will open another drop down menu from which you can choose a new role. Choose the type of permission that you need to grant to the user, then click the "SAVE" button.

You will have successfully added a new role to the user. If you go to the previous page, you will find that the role has been added to the other role.

Revoking Roles

Sometimes, you may need to revoke the roles that you have granted to a certain user. This can be done by following the steps given below:

Begin by clicking the Navigation Menu button from the main dashboard, choose "IAM & admin" then choose "IAM".

Ensure that you have chosen and opened the project you need to use.

Identify the member from whom you need to revoke the role. Move to the right icon then click the edit icon that looks like a pen/pencil.

A new pane will appear from which you can revoke the role from the user. The pane will show the roles that have been assigned to the user, making it easy for you to remove the role you no longer want the user to hold.

Identify the role that you want to revoke from the user, and then click the delete icon located to the right of the role. In my case, I want to revoke the "Editor" role from the user, so I will click the following icon:

Edit permissions

Member	Project
victorjohn979@gmail.com	App Engine Project

Role
App Engine Viewer ▾
Ability to view App Engine app status.

Role
Editor ▾
Edit access to all resources.

+ ADD ANOTHER ROLE

SAVE   CANCEL

The role will disappear immediately after clicking the delete icon. To save the changes, click the SAVE button located at the bottom of the pane. You will be taken back to the project's page, and you will be able to see that the role has been revoked successfully from the user.

You have successfully revoked the role from the user.

Granting Access to More Projects

You may decide to grant a certain member access to more than one project. This is possible in the GCP and it can be done as follows:

Begin by clicking the Navigation Menu button from the main dashboard, choose "IAM & admin" then choose "IAM".

Choose all the projects for which you need to grant the user access to.

Click "Show Info Panel" then click the "Permissions" tab to open it.

Enter the active email address of the user then choose their role from the drop down menu.

Click the "Add" button. The member will then be granted the role that you have selected to each of the projects you had chosen.

Note that once you grant a member a role via their email address, no email will be sending to them, but they will be activated immediately.

Chapter 5- Cluster Administration

The GCP comes with the Kubernetes Engine that is good for cluster management. The Google Cloud Platform is however capable of handling the basic cluster administration tasks on your behalf. An example of such task is ringing-up a kubernetes powered cluster.

Creating a Cluster

In this section, we shall be guiding you on how to create a cluster on the Kubernetes Engine.
The first step should be to enable the Kubernetes Engine API. This can be enabled from the Google Cloud Platform.

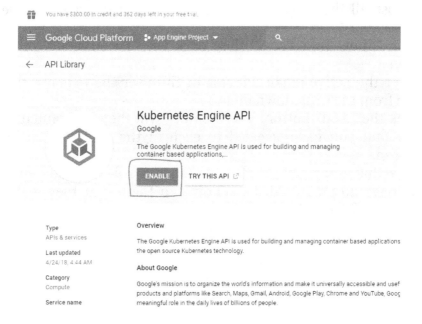

You should also install the Cloud SDK. This will come with tools such as gsutil, gcloud and the bq command line tools.
You also need to set the project ID. Note that the project name is different from the project ID. The project name is a human readable way of identifying your projects, but the Google APIs does not use the project ID. The project ID is generated at the time of creation of the project.

To know the ID for your project, you only have to go to the HOME page of your Google Cloud account. Just click the Navigation Menu button, and then choose HOME. You will be there!

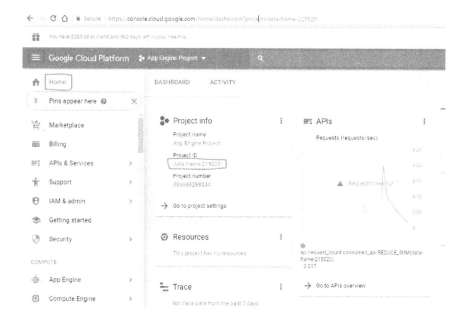

You can see the project dashboard has both the project name and the project ID.

To set the project ID, you should run the following command on the Google Cloud console:

gcloud config set project [PROJECT-ID]

To access the Google Console, click the icon for "Activate Cloud Shell" from the Home of your Google Cloud account. In my case, I run the command as follows:

gcloud config set project data-frame-215020

```
nicholassamuel1107@cloudshell:~ (data-frame-215020)$ gcloud config set project data-frame-215020
Updated property [core/project].
nicholassamuel1107@cloudshell:~ (data-frame-215020)$ 
```

Make sure you substitute your project ID in the command.

The next step should be to set the default compute zone. The available time zones can be obtained from the following URL: https://cloud.google.com/compute/docs/regions-zones/#available
To set the default time zone, run the following command:

gcloud config set compute/zone [COMPUTE-ZONE]

In my case, I run the following command:

gcloud config set compute/zone us-east1-b

```
nicholassamuel1107@cloudshell:~ (data-frame-215020)$ gcloud config set compute/zone us-east1-b
Updated property [compute/zone].
nicholassamuel1107@cloudshell:~ (data-frame-215020)$ []
```

You should also run the following command to ensure that all the gcloud commands are updated:
gcloud components update
The Kubernetes Engine allows you to create four types of clusters. These include Zonal clusters, Regional clusters, Private clusters or Alpha clusters.
A zonal cluster can be run on more than one compute zones within one region. A multi-zone cluster is the one that runs its nodes in two or even more compute zones in one region. Zonal clusters usually run one cluster master.
After creating a multi-zonal cluster, either a new one or through addition of zones to an existing cluster, the Kubernetes Engine will make the resource footprint similar in all zones.
An example is when you request for two nodes each with four cores, and you request to be spread across a total of three zones. In such a case, you will get 24 cores, each zone having eight cores.
Multi-zone clusters are able to spread the resources across many zones evenly to ensure that the Pods are scheduled in an effective way across the zones.

This will improve failure recovery and availability. If the computing resources are not spread evenly across the zones, the scheduler will not be capable of scheduling the Pods evenly.

How to Create a Single-Zone Cluster

The gcloud command-line tool can be used for the purpose of creating a cluster.

This can be done by running the "gcloud container clusters" command.

The command takes the syntax given below:

gcloud container clusters create [CLUSTER-NAME] [--zone [COMPUTE-ZONE]]

The CLUSTER-NAME is the name you need to use for the cluster.

The –zone flag is optional and it overrides the default compute/zone property that is set by running the "gcloud config set compute/zone" command.

Here is an example that shows how to create a cluster named cluster12 in the east1-b zone:

gcloud container clusters create cluster12 --zone us-east1-b

The creation of the cluster may take some time, so be patient as the command runs.

```
Creating cluster cluster12...done.
Created [https://container.googleapis.com/v1/projects/data-frame-215020/zones/us-east1-b/clusters/cluster12].
To inspect the contents of your cluster, go to: https://console.cloud.google.com/kubernetes/workload_/gcloud/us-east1-b/cluster12?pro
kubeconfig entry generated for cluster12.
NAME       LOCATION    MASTER VERSION  MASTER IP      MACHINE TYPE  NODE VERSION  NUM NODES  STATUS
cluster12  us-east1-b  1.9.7-gke.6     35.237.146.147 n1-standard-1 1.9.7-gke.6   3          RUNNING
nicholassamuel1107@cloudshell:~ (data-frame-215020)$ []
```

The above figure shows that the cluster has been created.

You can also create the same cluster from the Console. To do this, click the Navigation menu button located at the dashboard. Scroll down to where we have "Kubernetes Engine", and click it.

Choose "Clusters" from the available options.

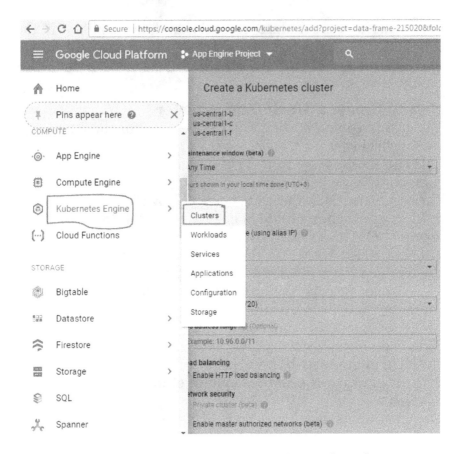

Click the "CREATE CLUSTER" button located at the top. You will be taken to a new page where you can fill in the details of the cluster.

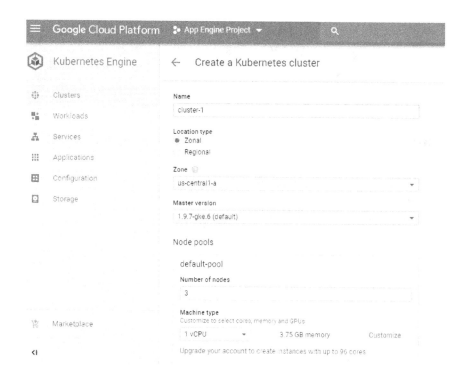

Here are the details that are required to fill:

Name- this is the name that you want to use for the cluster. This name should be unique within the project and zone.

Zone- this is the compute zone for the Compute Engine where you want to create the cluster.

Cluster size- this denotes the number of nodes that are to be created within the cluster. You should have available resource quota for nodes and resources like firewall routes.

Machine type- This is the Compute Engine machine type that is to be used for the instances. Note that billing is done differently for each machine type. The n1-standard-1 forms the default machine type.

Once you have filled all the details, click the "Create" button to complete the creation of the cluster.

How to Create a Multi-Zone Cluster

When creating a multi-zone cluster, you should use the –zone flag to define the zone for the cluster's control plane. All the required zones can be specified via the "-node.locations" flag. The command for creating a multi-zone cluster should take the syntax given below:

**gcloud container clusters create [CLUSTER-NAME] \
--zone [COMPUTE-ZONE] \
--node-locations   [COMPUTE-ZONE,COMPUTE-ZONE,...]`**

The CLUSTER-NAME is the name of the cluster that is to be created. The ---zone [COMPUTE-ZONE] denotes the zone for the control panel of the cluster. The --node-locations [COMPUTE-ZONE, COMPUTE-ZONE,...] denotes all the zones in which the cluster will run, including the zone for the cluster control pane. Here is an example of how we can create a multi-zone cluster:

**gcloud container clusters create cluster22 \
--zone us-east1-b \
--node-locations us-east1-b, us-central1-a,us-central1-c**

The command may take some minutes to complete, so remain patient until it is done.

We have specified three zones for the cluster. The default number of nodes per zone is 3. This means that the above command will create a nine-node cluster, with each zone having three nodes.

Regional Clusters

These types of clusters distribute the Kubernetes resources across many zones in a region. A regional cluster will create three cluster masters in three zones, and by default, nodes will be created in three zones, or in multiple zones as required.

A Regional Cluster can be created via GCP console or via gcloud command line tool. The default setting is that after the creation of a regional cluster, the node pools for the cluster will be replicated across the three zones. A regional cluster can be created by running the following command:

**gcloud container clusters create [CLUSTER-NAME]--region [REGION] **
[--node-locations [ZONE1,ZONE2...]`]

The CLUSTER-NAME is the name of the cluster to be created. The REGION is the region you need to cluster to run in. The "—node-locations" will override the default zones in which the clusters have been replicated.

Consider the example given below:

gcloud container clusters create cluster33 --region us-west1

The above command creates a cluster named cluster33 with nodes in the us-west1 region. There are three zones each with three nodes.

If you need to create some regional cluster having six nodes, that is, three zones each having two nodes; you can use the "—num-nodes" flag to specify this as shown below:

**gcloud container clusters create cluster33 --num-nodes 2 **
--region us-west1

The following command can help you create a regional cluster having six nodes in 2 zones. Each node will have three nodes. We can specify this via the "—node-locations" flag as shown below:

**gcloud container clusters create cluster44 --region us-central1 **
--node-locations us-central1-b, us-central1-c

You can also create a regional cluster via the console. First, open the Kubernetes Engine menu in GCP console. Click the button written "CREATE CLUSTER":

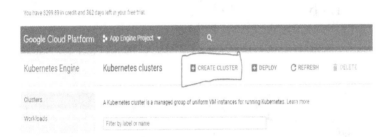

You will be directed to another page where you can enter the details of the Kubernetes cluster that you need to create.

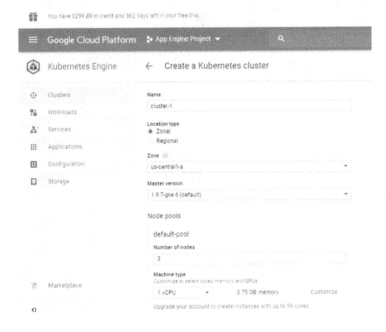

Enter the details of the cluster. For the Location section, select "Regional". You will be provided with a dropdown from where you should choose the region that you want. Once you have filled all the cluster details, click the "Create" button and the cluster will be created.

Alpha Clusters

These are short-lived clusters that usually run stable Kubernetes releases with features enabled. An alpha cluster can be created by running the following command:

**gcloud container clusters create [CLUSTER-NAME] **

--enable-kubernetes-alpha [--zone [COMPUTE-ZONE]]

[--cluster-version [VERSION]]

The CLUSTER-NAME is the name for the cluster you need to create. The COMPUTE-ZONE represents the Compute Engine in which you need to create the cluster. The "—zone" flag which is optional will override the default compute/zone property that was set by the gcloud config set compute/zone. The VERSION denotes the version of Kubernetes Engine that is to run in your cluster. Here is an example showing how to create an alpha cluster:

**gcloud container clusters create cluster55 **

--enable-kubernetes-alpha --zone us-central1-b — cluster-version 1.10

To know when your alphas cluster expires, run the following command:

gcloud container clusters list

```
nicholassamuel1107@cloudshell:~ (data-frame-215020)$ gcloud container clusters list
NAME       LOCATION   MASTER VERSION   MASTER IP        MACHINE TYPE   NODE VERSION   NUM NODES   STATUS
cluster1   us-east1-b  1.9.7-gke.6     35.196.197.39    n1-standard-1  1.9.7-gke.6    3           RUNNING
cluster12  us-east1-b  1.9.7-gke.6     35.237.146.147   n1-standard-1  1.9.7-gke.6    3           RUNNING
cluster33  us-west1    1.9.7-gke.6     35.197.126.12    n1-standard-1  1.9.7-gke.6    6           RUNNING
nicholassamuel1107@cloudshell:~ (data-frame-215020)$
```

43

The alpha cluster can also be created from the console. To do this, first open the menu for the Kubernetes Engine on the console. Identify the "CREATE CLUSTER" button from the top of the window and click it.

From the drop-down menu for the Master Version, choose the version of Kubernetes Engine that you want to use for the cluster. Configure the other cluster details as you desire.

In the section for Advanced Options, enable the option for "Enable Kubernetes alpha features in this cluster". If you get a warning, acknowledge the warning by choosing "I understand the consequences".

Once you have filled all the details, click the "Create" button to create the cluster.

Managing Clusters

Now that you have known how to create the various types of clusters, it will be good for you to know how to manage them.

To view the details of a specific cluster, run the following command:

gcloud container clusters describe [CLUSTER-NAME] –zone [ZONE]

For example, to view the details of a cluster named "cluster11", we run the following command:

gcloud container clusters describe cluster1 --zone us-east1-b

This returns the following:

```
nicholassamuel1107@cloudshell:~ (data-frame-215020)$ gcloud container clusters describe cluster1 --zone us-east1-b
addonsConfig:
  networkPolicyConfig:
    disabled: true
clusterIpv4Cidr: 10.16.0.0/14
createTime: '2018-09-03T10:46:02+00:00'
currentMasterVersion: 1.9.7-gke.6
currentNodeCount: 3
```

Note that above is just a section of the output, but the command returns more output that shown above.

If you want to view the details of all the available clusters, you just run the command we used previously as shown below:

gcloud container clusters list

You may need to set the default cluster for the gcloud commands. To do this, use the command given below:

gcloud config set container/cluster [CLUSTER-NAME]

The CLUSTER-NAME is the name of the cluster that you want to set as the default.

It is also possible for us to add or remove cluster zones. This can be done using the command "gcloud container clusters update" which takes the syntax given below:

**gcloud container clusters update [CLUSTER-NAME] \
--zone [COMPUTE-ZONE] \
--node-locations [COMPUTE-ZONE, COMPUTE-ZONE,...]**

The cluster named "cluster1" is running in one zone only, that is, us-east1-b. We can add two additional zones to the cluster by running the command given below:

**gcloud container clusters update cluster1 \
--zone us-east1-b \
--node-locations us-east1-b, us-west1**

Other than running a command, you can use the graphical user interface provided by the console.

To do this, open the menu for the Kubernetes Engine in the GCP Console.

You can see that the list of all the clusters that you have in the Engine are shown. Identify the cluster who zone you need to change then select it. Click edit, which is the icon that looks like a pen/pencil to the far right of the cluster name.

In the above case, I want to change the zone for the cluster named cluster1.

Scroll down to the section for "Additional Zones". Select the zones that you need to add the cluster to.

Once done with the selection of the zones, scroll downwards then click the "Save" button to save the changes. The changes will be applied to the cluster successfully.

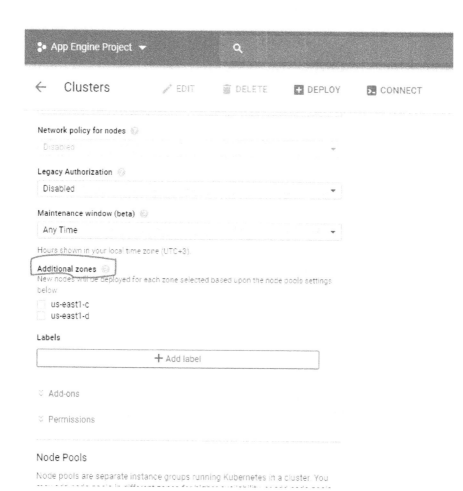

Chapter 6- Storage

Your Compute Engine instances are provided with a number of storage options.

The default setting is that every instance of the Compute Engine has one root persistent disk that has the operating system. In case your application is in need of an additional storage space, you have the ability to add one or more storage options to the instance. Other that the storage options provided by the Google Cloud Platform, it is possible for you to deploy alternative storage options to your instance. Here are examples of such alternatives:

You can create a distributed file system or a file server on the Compute Engine to use network file system with SMB3 and NFSv3 capabilities.

You can also mount a RAM disk within the instance memory to come up with a block storage volume with low latency and high throughput.

The block storage options are known to have different characteristics in terms of performance. You must consider your performance requirements and storage size to be able to determine the right type of block storage for your instances.

Zonal Persistent Disks

Persistent disks refer to durable network storage devices that the instances may access in the same way as physical disks in server or desktop computers. The Compute Engine is responsible for managing the data distribution and the persistence disks to ensure there is redundancy and optimize the performance on your behalf. The standard persistent disks are usually backed by the standard hard disk drives (HDD). The SSD persistent disks are usually backed by the solid state drives (SDD).

The persistent disks are located independently from the instances of the virtual machine, meaning that it is possible for you to detach the persistent disks to retain your data even after deletion of the instances.

The performance of the persistent disk will scale automatically with the size, meaning that it is possible for you to resize the existing persistent disks or even add more persistent disks to the instance so as to meet your storage and performance requirements.
The following steps can help you create a persistent disk for your instance:
On the main dashboard of your Google Cloud account, click the Navigation menu button; choose Compute Engine and then "VM Instances".

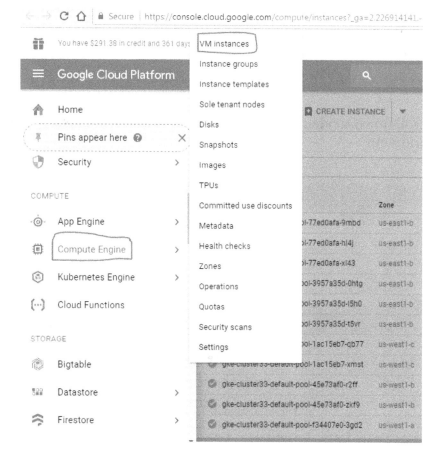

You will be taken to a page with all the instances that you have. Identify the instance to which you need to add the disk.

You will be taken to the page showing the instance details. At the top of this page, click the "EDIT" button:

Scroll down to identify the section for "Additional disks". Click "Add item".

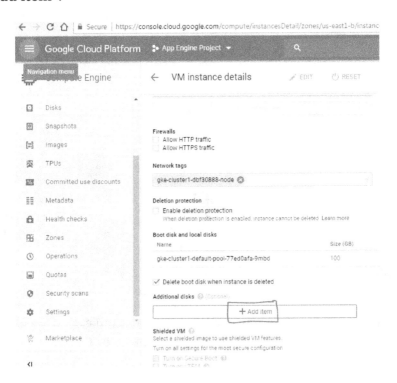

In the drop down box for "Name", choose "Create disk". New page will popup.

Enter the dame for the disk and configure the other disk details. Ensure that you have selected the option for "Blank disk".

Once you have filled in all the disk details, click the "Create" button to create the disk.

At the end of the page, click the "Save" button to save all the changes you have made.

Once you have created and attached a new disk to any instance, you should format then mount the disk for the operating system to use the available storage space.

The Compute Engine normally encrypts your data before it can travel outside your instance into the persistent disk storage space. Every persistent disk will stay encrypted with either system-defined keys or customer-supplied keys.

Also, Google normally distributes the persistent disk data across many physical disks in a way that the users don't control.

After the deletion of a persistent disk, Google will discard the cipher keys, and the data will be rendered irretrievable. This process cannot be reversed. If you need to exercise control over the keys that were used to encrypt the data, you should create your disk and your encryption keys.

Regional Persistent Disks

Regional persistent disks are known to possess storage qualities that are the same to both SSD and Standard persistent disks. However, the regional persistent disks have an advantage in that they provide a durable storage as well as replication of data across two zones located in the same region. If you are in need of developing a robust system within the Compute Engine, it is recommended that you use a regional persistent disk to maintain a high availability of resources across the zones. They also provide synchronous replication for workloads which may not have the application-level replication.

The regional persistent disks have been designed to be used in workloads that need redundancy across many zones with failover capabilities. They are also good for use with the regional managed instance groups. They are ban option for enterprise applications and high performance databases that also need high availability.

In case a zonal outage occurs, you may failover the workload running on the regional persistent disk to another zone by running the "force-attach command". This command will allow you to attach the regional persistent disk to some standby instance of VM even if it is not possible to detach the disk from the original VM as a result of its unavailability.

A write will only be acknowledged back in the VM only if it is durably persistent in the two parties. In case of unavailability of one of the replicas, the Compute Engine will only write to healthy replica. After a backup of the unhealthy replica, it will be transparently brought into sync with the healthy one and a fully synchronous mode of operation will resume.

In any case the two replicas become unavailable at once, or in case the healthy one disappears while the unhealthy one is being synced, the disk will become unavailable.

The following steps will help you add a regional persistent disk:

On the main dashboard of your Google Cloud Platform account, click the Navigation menu button to open the left navigation bar. Click the option for "Compute Engine" then choose "Disks". This will open the disks page.

Choose the project you need to use from the drop down located at the top then click "CREATE DISK".

Give the disk a name and choose the type of disk you want it to be.
Check the box for "Replicate this disk within region".
Choose the right region. Ensure that you mark this region since you are expected to choose the same region when you create the instance. You can write it down.

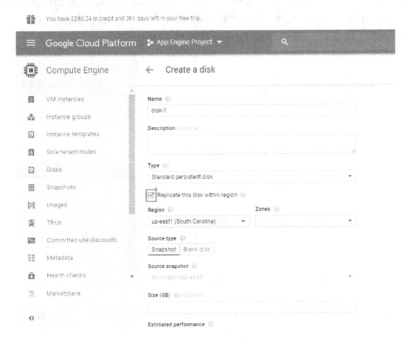

Choose two zones from the region, then click the OK button. Note that you must choose two zones. Again, ensure that you note the zones well as you will need the same to attach the disk to the instance in any of the zones.
Select the "Source Type".
Choose the "Encryption".
Click "Create" to complete the process of creating the disk.
Once you have created the regional persistent disk, you need to attach it to the instance. When attaching a disk to a cluster, you may get an error if the disk is already attached to another cluster.

You may be needed to force-attach the disk to instance via the Force-attach box located in the drop down box for "Additional disks".

Once a new disk is attached to an instance, you are required to format and mount the disk for the operating system to use the storage space that is available.

Local SSDs

These are physically attached to the server hosting the instance of virtual machine. Local SSDs are known for their low latency and higher throughput compared to SSD persistent disks and standard persistent disks. The data kept in a local SSD will persist until when the instance is deleted or stopped. Every local SSD has a size of 375 GB, but you are allowed to attach up to a maximum of 8 local SSD devices.

Instances with local SSD should be created when you have a workload that is distributed across many instances.

The Google Cloud Platform Console allows us to create an instance having a local SSD. To do this, follow the steps given below:

Click the Navigation menu button from the dashboard of your account. Click Compute Engine then choose "VM instances".

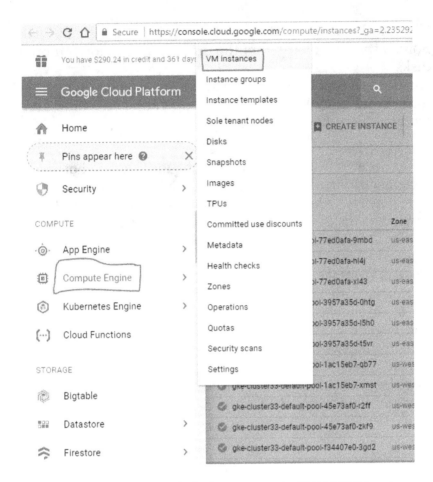

At the top of the screen, click "CREATE INSTANCE" button.

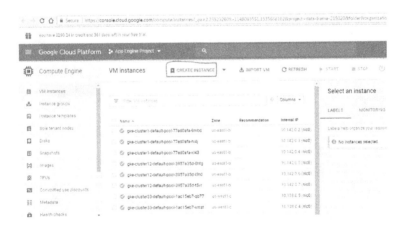

You will be taken to a page where you should fill in the required details for the instance. Just fill in the details for the instance.

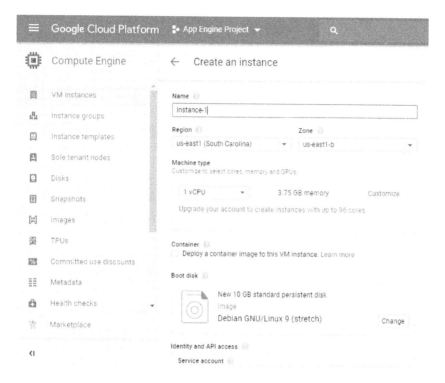

Expand the sections for Management, disks, security, networking, sole tenancy.

Click Disks then under Additional disks, click the button for "Add new disk".

Type the name of the disk in the Name field.

Under the "Type", select "Local SSD scratch disk (maximum 8)".

Click the button written "Done".

You can then the "Create" button to create the instance.

Once the local SSD has been created, you should format then mount the device before using it.

Conclusion

This marks the end of this book. The Google Cloud Platform is a cloud computing platform provided by Google. It provides its users with a number of services that are needed to manage data. The cloud is a safe and secure way of storing data. It relieves the burden of having to manage data on your own. There are a number of cloud providers that you will find in the market, but Google Cloud stands out to be the best. If you want to secure your company data, choose Google cloud.

The GCP is known to provide its users with flexible terms of payment. This is not the case with several other cloud computing platforms. It also has the capability of scaling up and down based on your requirements, and if such happens, you are only required to pay for the resources that you use. Data analysis is very essential to companies. The reason is that they can extract intelligence from the data which can be applied in decision making. When decisions are made based on intelligence, the company will have higher chances of success. The GCP provides Big Data and Machine Learning features which can be used for this. The GCP is a nice cloud computing platform I would recommend to any individual, business, company or organization.